Facts About the Frilled Lizard

The Frilled Dragon

By Lisa Strattin

© 2016 Lisa Strattin

Revised 2022 © Lisa Strattin

FREE BOOK

FREE FOR ALL SUBSCRIBERS

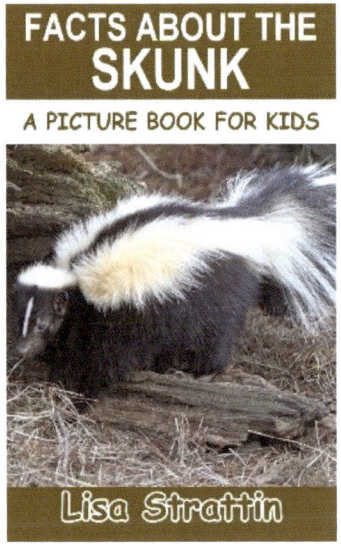

LisaStrattin.com/Subscribe-Here

BOX SET

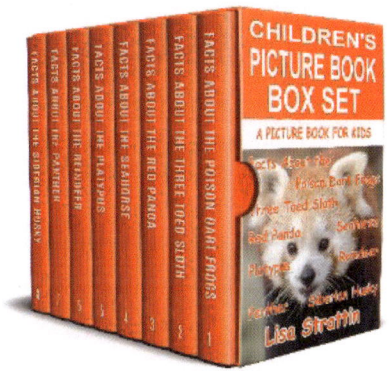

- **FACTS ABOUT THE POISON DART FROGS**
- **FACTS ABOUT THE THREE TOED SLOTH**
  - **FACTS ABOUT THE RED PANDA**
  - **FACTS ABOUT THE SEAHORSE**
  - **FACTS ABOUT THE PLATYPUS**
  - **FACTS ABOUT THE REINDEER**
  - **FACTS ABOUT THE PANTHER**
- **FACTS ABOUT THE SIBERIAN HUSKY**

LisaStrattin.com/BookBundle

Facts for Kids Picture Books by Lisa Strattin

Little Blue Penguin, Vol 92

Chipmunk, Vol 5

Frilled Lizard, Vol 39

Blue and Gold Macaw, Vol 13

Poison Dart Frogs, Vol 50

Blue Tarantula, Vol 115

African Elephants, Vol 8

Amur Leopard, Vol 89

Sabre Tooth Tiger, Vol 167

Baboon, Vol 174

Sign Up for New Release Emails Here

LisaStrattin.com/subscribe-here

All rights reserved. No part of this book may be reproduced by any means whatsoever without the written permission from the author, except brief portions quoted for purpose of review.

All information in this book has been carefully researched and checked for factual accuracy. However, the author and publisher makes no warranty, express or implied, that the information contained herein is appropriate for every individual, situation or purpose and assume no responsibility for errors or omissions. The reader assumes the risk and full responsibility for all actions, and the author will not be held responsible for any loss or damage, whether consequential, incidental, special or otherwise, that may result from the information presented in this book.

All images are free for use or purchased from stock photo sites or royalty free for commercial use.

Some coloring pages might be of the general species due to lack of available images.

I have relied on my own observations as well as many different sources for this book and I have done my best to check facts and give credit where it is due. In the event that any material is used without proper permission, please contact me so that the oversight can be corrected.

★★COVER IMAGE★★

https://www.flickr.com/photos/141679113@N08/47183497041/

★★ADDITIONAL IMAGES★★

https://www.flickr.com/photos/httpwwwflickrcomphotostopend/3212685830

https://www.flickr.com/photos/sussexbirder/8603083622/

https://www.flickr.com/photos/alexpanoiu/20858885288/

https://www.flickr.com/photos/24931020@N02/8541292065/

https://www.flickr.com/photos/yvonne81/3574796541/

https://www.flickr.com/photos/naparazzi/2715154286/

https://www.flickr.com/photos/141679113@N08/51052940278/

https://www.flickr.com/photos/walkn/2416229884/

https://www.flickr.com/photos/g_kat26/5636885440/

https://www.flickr.com/photos/edenpictures/51200646577/

Contents

INTRODUCTION 9
APPEARANCE AND CHARACTERISTICS..... 11
SIZE 13
HABITAT 15
DIET 17
EGGS TO HATCHLING 19
SOCIAL BEHAVIOR... 21
SUITABILITY AS PETS 25

INTRODUCTION

The Frilled Lizard also known as the *Frilled Dragon*, is a species found mainly in northern Australia and southern New Guinea. Its common name comes from the large frill around its neck, which usually stays folded against the lizard's body.

Today these magnificent lizards are commercially bred in large numbers–both on farms in Indonesia and by herptoculturists (reptile specialists and breeders) worldwide. Although not an easy species to keep as a pet, these frilled dragons are among the most rewarding lizards to have and will provide you with a lifetime of interest and enjoyment.

APPEARANCE AND CHARACTERISTICS

Male Frilled Lizards are more brightly colored than the females. The overall pattern as well as the color of its skin depends on where it lives. This is known as camouflage. Frilled Lizards in Queensland are yellow with black and white markings while those in the Northern Territory are orange with red, black, and white speckles.

There are two long, pointed canine-like teeth present in the lower jaw, which can inflict a painful bite. Since it has excellent camouflage characteristics, it is usually observed only when it descends to the ground after a rainfall or to search for food.

SIZE

The frill- lizard is a relatively large reptile, with males averaging around 3 feet in length in Australia and just over 2 feet in length in New Guinea (including the tail.) The females are about 2/3 the length of the males.

It is the second largest lizard in the family Agamidae, second only to the sailfin dragon.

HABITAT

These lizards inhabit humid climates such as those in tropical savannah woodlands. The Frilled Lizard spends a majority of its time up in the trees. They venture to the ground only in search of food, or to fight in territorial conflicts. The trees are most importantly used for camouflage.

Frilled lizards breed during the dry season when food is scarcer. During the breeding season, larger males will engage in dramatic territorial displays in an effort to attract the smaller females and scare off potential rivals.

At the onset of the wet season, mature females will deposit up to two dozen eggs. The eggs are buried in the ground and then left unattended to hatch on their own.

Frilled dragons mature over two to three years and are known to live up to 20 years in captivity as pets.

DIET

Like many lizards, Frilled Lizards are carnivores, feeding on cicadas, beetles, termites, and mice. They especially favor butterflies, moths, and love their larvae even more.

Though insects are their primary source of food, they also eat spiders and occasionally other lizards. Like most members of the dragon family, Frilled Lizards ambush prey, lying in wait for them. When the lizards eat, they eat a lot at one time; these binge periods usually happen during the wet season, when they eat hundreds to thousands of flying ants or termites.

EGGS TO HATCHLING

Females might lay 8 to 23 tiny eggs at one time in an underground nest. The hatchlings emerge fully independent and capable of hunting and showing off its frilled neck.

SOCIAL BEHAVIOR

Frilled Dragons are much more tolerant of being kept in a pair or group than some other dragons. Whereas Bearded Dragons should always be housed alone, Frilled Dragons can be placed in a confined area with several others. However, only one male should be in a group because the males will fight over the territory. When keeping lizards housed together, it is important to observe how they interact so that you can make sure they don't hurt one another.

Healthy captive-born juveniles are quite easy to raise together, but wild-caught or farm-raised animals may need separation due to stress as well as parasites they may have picked up during the importation process.

Lizards may look like they get along fine (they might sit or sleep on each other), but if one tries to hold on to the basking area (the warmer spot in the habitat) without allowing another one to join, there is a possibility that mental stress is harming the more submissive lizard. The submissive lizard might grow weak and die if it isn't separated from the more dominant cage mates.

SUITABILITY AS PETS

This is, to say the very least, not your average lizard!

For many people having one of these beauties as a pet is about as close as they will ever come to owning a real life dinosaur dragon, which is why you will sometimes see this species called the *"Frilled Dragon Lizard."*

Given that Frilled Dragons are territorial, it is also quite natural that they will instinctively feel stressed without enough space, even if they do have plenty of food and are protected from competing lizards.

Territorial animals almost always need the perception of an adequate space in which to live, despite the fact that their basic needs might, in captivity, be met in a fairly small area.

COLOR ME

COLOR ME

COLOR ME

COLOR ME

COLOR ME

COLOR ME

COLOR ME

COLOR ME

COLOR ME

COLOR ME

Please leave me a review here:

LisaStrattin.com/Review-Vol-39

For more Kindle Downloads Visit Lisa Strattin Author Page on Amazon Author Central

amazon.com/author/lisastrattin

To see upcoming titles, visit my website at LisaStrattin.com– most books available on Kindle!

LisaStrattin.com

FREE BOOK

FOR ALL SUBSCRIBERS – SIGN UP NOW

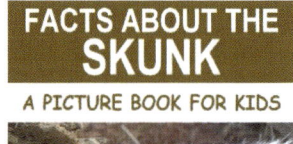

LisaStrattin.com/Subscribe-Here

LisaStrattin.com/Facebook

LisaStrattin.com/Youtube

Printed in Great Britain
by Amazon